FOCUS ON SAFETY

Recreation can be RISKY

BILL GUTMAN

Twenty-First Century Books
A Division of Henry Holt and Company/New York

For Cathy

Twenty-First Century Books
A Division of Henry Holt and Company, Inc.
115 West 18th Street
New York, NY 10011

Henry Holt® and colophon are trademarks of
Henry Holt and Company, Inc.
Publishers since 1866

Library of Congress Cataloging-in-Publication Data
Gutman, Bill.
Recreation can be risky / Bill Gutman.—1st ed.
p. cm.—(Focus on safety)
Includes index.
Summary: Shows how to prevent injuries and accidents during play and
recreational activities by exercising greater care and being less reckless.
1. Outdoor recreation—Safety measures—Juvenile literature. 2. Recreation—Safety
measures—Juvenile literature. [1. Outdoor recreation—Safety measures. 2. Play—
Safety measures. 3. Safety.] I. Title. II. Series: Gutman, Bill. Focus on safety.
GV191.625.G88 1996   95-40731
790'.028'9—dc20   CIP
                                                        AC

ISBN 0-8050-4143-5
First Edition 1996

Cover design by Robin Hoffman
Interior design by Kelly Soong

Printed in the United States of America
All first editions are printed on acid-free paper ∞.
10 9 8 7 6 5 4 3 2 1

Photo credits appear on page 80.

CONTENTS

FOREWORD

Safety is a simple, six-letter word that means being secure and protected from harm. Everyone would like to feel safe, every day of their lives. That would be an ideal situation.

Unfortunately, none of us lives in a perfect world. In reality, this is a world where there are risks and where accidents and other bad things happen. And they can happen anywhere and at any time.

Many of the things that put us in jeopardy, however, can be avoided if we become more aware of our surroundings. All of us must be able to identify conditions that may put us in danger and take measures to alter those conditions. In other words, we must practice prevention.

For an overall focus on safety to really work, it must become a way of life, something each person is aware of every day. The safety net must always be up. No one wants to become just another statistic. And we should be willing to do everything in our power to keep that from happening.

INTRODUCTION

Everyone has time for fun in their lives. None of us can work *all* the time, or study *all* the time, or even sit and watch television *all* the time. We simply want to get up, get out, and play.

Play for some kids might involve an organized sport like basketball, soccer, or football. It can be with a league or just a pickup sandlot game. For others, fun might mean biking or swimming. For still others, nothing can beat the adventure of skateboarding or in-line skating. Hiking, rock climbing, ice-skating, and traditional street games like tag and hide-and-seek are also popular activities kids enjoy in their spare time.

All of these activities are pastimes kids can enjoy while improving their health and fitness—a winning combination. But most vigorous and/or recreational physical activity has built-in risks.

Almost all sports fans have witnessed injuries during sporting events. Of course, some injuries are more serious than others. It's a fact that most professional athletes are hurt at some point in their careers. Professional athletes, however, are paid very well to play hard, and often with reckless abandon. Injuries are simply a part of the game.

Recreational athletes can be more careful. By taking a few, often simple, precautions they can greatly reduce the chances of getting hurt while they are having fun. That doesn't mean that you or any of your friends won't sustain a sports-related injury someday. Playing hard can lead to injury. But by knowing your limits and being careful, you can cut down the odds.

Let's take a quick look at some statistics compiled by the National Safety Council. They have recorded the number of injuries in various sports and recreational activities compared with the number of people participating in each activity. To be considered an injury, there must be a record of treatment in a hospital emergency room.

Swimming and bicycle riding have the most participants. In the last set of figures compiled by the National Safety Council in 1992, there were some 63.1 million people swimming in the United States. From that group came 122,697 injuries. Biking had 54.6 million riders with 649,536 injuries. That's a much higher percentage of injuries than for swimming.

Let's look at basketball, baseball and softball, and football next. Basketball had 28.2 million people taking part with 752,798 reported injuries. Baseball and softball had 34.3 million participants with 477,380 injuries, while football caused 447,320 injuries with just 13.5 million taking part.

Competitive team sports can lead to many injuries, but so can unsupervised street sports. In 1992, there were some 5.5 million skateboarders in the United States. Of that group, 44,068 were injured. At the same time, 26.5 million people were using roller skates or in-line skates. Of that number, there were 136,353 injuries, with 10,800 related specifically to in-line skates. The number of people injured on in-line skates, incidentally, has grown dramatically since.

You must keep in mind that these numbers reflect only injuries that required emergency-room treatment. There were countless others that were treated at home or by private doctors. So the number of people injured is much higher than these statistics indicate.

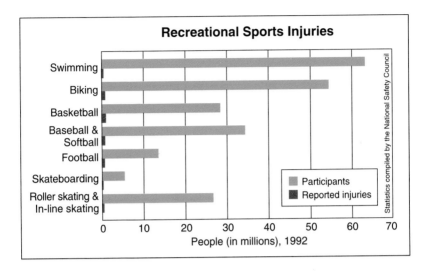

Recreational Sports Injuries

Statistics compiled by the National Safety Council

People (in millions), 1992

- Participants
- Reported injuries

No one leaves home in the morning for a day of biking, swimming, basketball, or skateboarding and expects to end up in the hospital before the day is done. Many recreational injuries and accidents can be prevented with a little less recklessness and a little more care.

TEAM SPORTS

In recent years, one of the highlights of television sports shows has been film clips showing hard-hitting collisions and other supposedly humorous sports bloopers. Unfortunately, these bloopers often result in someone being injured.

Sports injuries are nothing to laugh at—not at the professional level or in a sandlot pickup game. Injuries have shortened or ended a number of promising professional sports careers over the years. They have also sent many youngsters to the hospital. Some injuries are unavoidable. That's the nature of competitive team sports.

But there are some kinds of injuries that *can* be avoided. The more you know about playing your sport and the better you prepare, the less chance you'll have of getting hurt. This doesn't mean you shouldn't play hard. Sometimes it is safer to play hard than to hold back. Stay in the flow of the game, whether it's fast or slow.

Let's take a look at some of the sports that kids like to play and at the pitfalls you should watch out for.

BASEBALL AND SOFTBALL

There are two ways to play baseball or softball—with an organized team or on the sandlot with your friends. Organized ball might be played with a school or neighborhood team, YMCA club, Little League team, or Babe Ruth League team.

Organized teams usually have at least one coach and the right kind of equipment. *Sandlot* is a term for a bunch of kids just playing the game anywhere they want. It might just be two-a-cat with a few players, a regular game with nine on a side, or anything in between. Sandlot games are often played on poor fields and sometimes without the right kind of equipment. Chances are, if you like baseball, you'll play both organized and sandlot ball.

START BY BEING IN SHAPE *If you want to play, get in shape!* This is a rule to follow for all kinds of sports and physical activities. The more physical the sport, the better shape you should be in before you even start. In other words, don't go out and play a vigorous sport where you have to run, jump, swing your arms, or really stretch any part of your body if you haven't been doing any kind of physical activity.

You don't have to train like a professional athlete. But you must keep your body active, your muscles toned and stretched. If you do this by simply playing a lot of baseball or softball, that's fine. But if you've done nothing more than be a couch potato for three months and then decide to play a vigorous game of baseball, you're looking for trouble.

What can happen? Someone totally out of shape who plays baseball or softball can pull or strain a variety of muscles in the legs, groin, arms, or ribs. Rib pulls can result from swinging a bat too hard. They are painful and take a long time to heal. Leg pulls are sometimes caused by stopping and starting on the bases or simply by running as fast as you can. Groin pulls can result from stopping suddenly or from sliding incorrectly. Arm muscles can be strained from swinging the bat or throwing the ball too hard.

Kids who go out to play baseball for a few hours won't be too happy if they end up limping around for the next few weeks or having their ribs hurt every time they laugh or cough.

WHAT CAN YOU DO? If you're already playing baseball two or three times a week, chances are you're in good shape. But if you have been totally inactive, or involved in an unrelated activity like bike riding or basketball, you should begin to pay special attention to your "baseball muscles":

1. Always stretch your muscles before you begin. Do a series of stretching exercises for the legs and groin area, as well as for the arms and shoulders.
2. Start doing some basic calisthenics, such as push-ups, sit-ups, and pull-ups.
3. Combine distance jogging with some quick, stop-and-go sprints.
4. Begin throwing a baseball or softball on a regular basis. Don't throw hard at first, just lob it. Some soreness is to be expected.
5. Swing a bat every day. Swing easily for a while and then work up to some harder swings. That will get your shoulders, arms, and wrist muscles ready for the real thing.

A WARNING ABOUT PITCHING Pitching a baseball is an unnatural motion of the arm. Underhand softball pitching is close to a natural motion: it's a downward arc, almost like a natural swing of the arm and shoulder. But overhand pitching can put a tremendous strain on the shoulder and elbow.

Young players only have to look at the major leagues to see how many professional pitchers have arm and shoulder injuries. A number of outstanding careers have been cut short by the dreaded rotator cuff injury. The rotator cuff is a sheath of muscles in the shoulder. A tear of these muscles can be very painful, and can take months to heal. Sometimes surgery is required.

Young pitchers should start slowly and have a good coach to advise them. Don't throw too hard too soon. Your arm is still growing and developing. Young pitchers should also not try to throw curves, sliders, or screwballs. All of these pitches require snapping motions of the wrist, which put a big strain on the elbow.

If you like to pitch, start slowly and be careful. And if you feel any kind of pain in your arm, elbow, or shoulder, tell your coach about it. If you don't have a coach, tell your parents or guardians and see a doctor. *Never* continue to throw a baseball once your arm begins hurting.

PITFALLS ON THE DIAMOND If you play on an organized team, chances are you will have the right equipment and play on a good field. Catchers will have protective equipment (shin guards, chest protector, mask) and hitters will have batting helmets. There will also be coaches to show you the right way to hit, pitch, field, run the bases, and slide. All of these things help keep injuries to a minimum.

Sandlot ball can be a different story. Fields are sometimes just rutty, rocky pastures. Catchers don't always have the protection they need. Players often try sliding without proper instruction and on unsafe ground. Sure, you can have a great time. Many people still think sandlot ball is the essence of baseball. But it's also where injuries often occur.

To be safe, start by being aware of the following:

1. **Police the field before you play.** All the players should walk around both the infield and outfield. Remove loose stones and any sharp objects. If there is a deep hole, fill it with dirt. Stepping in a hole can cause a foot, ankle, or knee injury, or more. So get the field in the best shape possible.
2. **Wear the right clothes.** Never play baseball in shorts or bare feet. Playing in shorts can lead to scrapes and bruises if you slide or collide with another player. Playing in bare feet can lead to foot injuries. You can be stepped on by another player or you can step on a sharp object.
3. **Be careful sliding.** Sliding into a base looks easy, but it isn't. If

Sliding into a base incorrectly is one of the most frequent causes of injury to baseball players.

you don't slide the right way, you can easily injure an ankle, leg, or knee. Get some instruction before you slide and practice before you try it in a game.

FOOTBALL

Kids play two basic kinds of football—touch football and tackle football. Touch is the less physical game. To stop the ball carrier or pass receiver, or to keep the quarterback from throwing, you simply touch the player with one or two hands.

Tackle is a different story. Now the ball carrier must be taken to the ground—knocked or dragged down—to stop the play. There is fierce blocking on every play and hard-hitting collisions.

Statistics show that the injury rate in football is the highest of any team sport. With all the physical contact, that shouldn't be surprising. Yet football continues to be a popular sport, one that many kids enjoy playing. With tackle football, however, you've really got to get yourself ready if you're doing your best to avoid injuries.

STRENGTH, SPEED, CONDITION As with all sports, the better your physical condition, the better you will be able to perform. This is especially true for football. And the better your overall condition, the less chance you have of getting hurt. Even touch football can have pretty rough blocking and should not be taken lightly.

Anyone getting ready to play football should do the same types of basic exercises described for baseball. Serious football players also do some kind of strength training with weights or other types of muscle-building machines. But young athletes should do this only under the supervision of a coach or trainer, who will decide if they are old enough to begin such a training program.

SUPERVISED VERSUS UNSUPERVISED FOOTBALL   Unsupervised, or sandlot, tackle football can be a very dangerous sport. It's not as simple as a bunch of kids getting together to play sandlot baseball. In sandlot football, kids will often play without protective equipment, such as shoulder, hip, and knee pads and helmets. The lack of a helmet is the most serious problem. If you play tackle football without a helmet, you are risking a serious head injury. There are also games in which some players wear helmets and others do not. That's even worse, because the helmets can then be used as weapons.

Many of those participating in sandlot football games have had no coaching. They can make the mistake of trying to copy the pros, doing the things they see on television, especially those wild highlight films. This, too, can easily result in injury.

There are often no officials to enforce the rules in sandlot football games. If tempers flare, the game can get even rougher. It's one thing if a group of kids on a team want to play or practice on their own. But neighborhood "challenge" games should be organized and supervised.

Organized football often starts with the Pop Warner League, which is the equivalent of Little League in baseball. There, youngsters learn the fundamentals and play against opponents their same age and weight. They will have the proper equipment and supervision.

INJURIES ON THE GRIDIRON   No one can play football while afraid of getting injured. Yet almost everyone who plays the game is hurt once in a while. Football injuries include muscle pulls, especially of the hamstring; hand, wrist, ankle, knee, and shoulder injuries, and sometimes neck and head injuries. Report any small injury to your coach, trainer, parents, or guardians immediately. Do not practice or play if you are hurt. Playing with certain minor injuries can lead to a major injury. It isn't worth the risk.

Protective equipment can lessen a football player's risk of injury.

GOOD COACHING AND SPORTSMANSHIP

In the 1970s, Larry Csonka was the star fullback of the Miami Dolphins. "Zonk" was one of the best and toughest runners in the National Football League. One day, Csonka stopped to watch a Pop Warner League football game. During the action, one player suffered a hard blow to the nose. He lay on the ground in obvious pain, blood streaming from his nose.

Csonka was appalled to see the team's coach standing over the player, screaming at him to get up, be a man, forget about his injury, and get back in the game. The reaction of one of the most hard-nosed football players ever was that this man didn't belong in coaching. Certainly he should not have been coaching children. Not only was he taking the fun out of the game, he was risking further injury to the young player. And he was also doing the player possible emotional harm.

Team sports for youngsters should be fun. They can provide a way to gain new skills, to learn to compete, to practice being part of a team, and to show good sportsmanship. It's the job of a coach to work with his team, to teach all of these things. You try to win, but if you don't there will always be another day.

A coach is also supposed to look out for the health and well-being of the players. The coach should not verbally or physically abuse them in the name of being tough. If you think your coach is bringing the wrong qualities to the job, tell your parents or guardians about it.

A bad coach can not only take the fun out of a sport, but can also expose you to physical danger and injury.

BASKETBALL

Basketball has become *the* game for kids of all ages in both cities and rural areas. Hoops are appearing in more and more driveways and backyards, in playgrounds, and even on street corners. In fact, many feel that basketball will soon become the most popular sport in the entire world!

Basketball can be played alone or by a full ten players, five to a side. Anything in between goes, as well. There are many organized leagues—in schools, parks, playgrounds, YMCAs, and church groups. In addition, there are countless numbers of pickup games going on across the country every day.

Millions of boys and girls play basketball as a recreational activity. It's fun, healthful, and competitive. But, like other sports, playing basketball can result in injuries. By preparing yourself to play, you can avoid or lessen many of these potential injuries.

PLAYING AT FULL THROTTLE It's been said that basketball is a game of running and jumping, speed, and quickness. The game is often played at full throttle, with players changing direction quickly many times as they switch from offense to defense. To play basketball, you've got to be in top physical condition.

Everyone who plays basketball should do a lot of running. If you play almost every day, just the game itself will keep you in shape. But if you're not in shape and get tired, that's when injuries can occur.

Unlike other sports, you don't need a lot of special equipment to play hoops. Just a good pair of basketball shoes (sneakers), high or low cut, should do it. Make sure the shoes fit properly. They shouldn't be too loose or too tight. Then you're ready to go.

PITFALLS ON THE COURT Played hard, basketball has more physical contact than some people think. Players fighting for

GET YOURSELF GOOD GOGGLES

If you wear eyeglasses or contact lenses and play a team sport—especially a contact sport or a sport that involves a ball of some kind—you should take some extra precautions. The best thing is to wear safety goggles especially designed for athletic competition.

These goggles are padded to protect the area around the eyes and the eyes themselves from a blow. There is usually an elastic strap to keep them in place.

There are two types of athletic goggles you can obtain. The first is the nonprescription type. They simply protect the eyes and can be worn over contact lenses. The second type are prescription goggles, with your eyeglass prescription in the lenses. Either way, goggles offer excellent eye protection and do not obscure your vision.

Even professional athletes use goggles to protect their eyes. Kareem Abdul-Jabbar wore goggles before he retired from the National Basketball Association.

rebounds slam into one another. Players driving to the basket can be fouled hard. It's not unusual to see two or three players diving for a loose ball. Hands, arms, and elbows are often flailing about on the court. All of these things can lead to injury.

Common basketball injuries include sprained ankles, jammed or sprained fingers, and a finger or elbow in the eye. Knee, elbow, shoulder, back, and head injuries aren't as common, but can happen. The more serious injuries often happen when a player is hit after he jumps high in the air. Some of the best players jump so high that their legs can be cut out from under them. Depending on how they land, they can be badly injured.

As with other competitive sports, there's no way to avoid every injury. Being in top physical condition and improving your skill level will help. On the court, try to keep your body in full control. Sometimes, however, competitive instinct will take over and you'll find yourself diving for a loose ball and leaping into the air without full control. That kind of competitiveness is part of being an athlete and also part of the risk.

A WORD ABOUT PICKUP GAMES   Pickup games in basketball are very common. Kids will often play three-on-three at a local playground with the winners staying on the court and the losers leaving. It's like one challenge after another. The players are often very skilled and the games hard-fought. And there usually is no referee.

Without fouls being called by a ref, pickup games can get very rough, with more injuries than usual. A hard foul will usually lead to a harder foul. Rules can be violated and tempers sometimes flare. That makes the players even more exposed to injury or to a fight.

Try to keep pickup games under control. Don't allow yourself to be baited by trash talk and don't do any trash talking yourself. Let your athletic ability make your statement.

A DANGEROUS SHORTCUT

To be the best they can be, athletes must be in top physical condition. In most sports, this means a combination of strength, speed, and agility. Athletes often look for every possible way to get an edge, to be just a little bit better than their opponents.

Unfortunately, getting an edge has resulted in the use of illegal and/or harmful drugs by some athletes. One of the most dangerous groups of drugs used by athletes is called anabolic steroids. *Webster's Sports Dictionary* defines an anabolic steroid as "any of a group of usually synthetic hormones that increase constructive metabolism and that are sometimes taken by athletes in training in order to increase the size of their muscles temporarily."

There are some steroids that are prescribed by doctors and have bona fide medical use. The steroids taken by athletes to build muscle are not only illegal, but they can also have devastating side effects. Perhaps the most famous victim of steroid abuse was former all-pro defensive tackle Lyle Alzado, who was a National Football League star for more than a decade. Alzado

SOCCER

Soccer has become a widespread organized sport for youngsters in the United States. There are age-group leagues everywhere. These leagues are usually well supervised and well coached. But anytime you get a bunch of players all trying to head and kick a ball, injuries can happen.

A soccer player is going to do a lot of running. That's why the sport is a very healthy one for young athletes. You cannot died of brain cancer in 1992 at the age of forty-three. Before he died, he told anyone who would listen that he felt his longtime use and abuse of steroids caused his illness.

Football players, body builders, professional wrestlers, and track and field performers are among the many athletes who have used steroids to build muscle and improve performance. It is now known that steroids can also cause liver and kidney damage and induce personality and mood changes. *Steroid rage* is a term used to describe sudden periods of violent behavior by steroid abusers.

Young athletes should be especially aware of any kind of performance-enhancing supplements they are offered. Someone might tell you the pills they are offering are special vitamins when, in reality, they are steroids. Steroids are simply something no one should fool with, not even for a short period of time.

Do not take any kind of pill or liquid supplement unless you are absolutely sure what you are taking. If you have a question, ask an adult or a doctor. Steroids are very dangerous. Don't let anyone tell you otherwise.

play if you are out of shape. A tired player can get hurt more easily. So always make sure you're ready to run a lot when you join a team. That may mean running on your own before you start and even during the season, in addition to your games.

THE RIGHT EQUIPMENT Soccer is a very basic sport. The ball is the main piece of equipment. Players should wear light and loose shirts and shorts so they can move freely. A good supportive pair of shoes is also essential. For most fields, coaches will suggest soccer shoes with some kind of cleats. Some players will wear shin guards and even knee pads. Goal posts should be padded, too!

The percentage of injuries occurring in soccer is less than the other sports discussed in this book. There are bruises from being accidentally kicked, turned ankles, occasional knee injuries, and other injuries from falls.

As with other sports, don't do more than your skill level allows. For example, if you haven't practiced an overhead scissors kick, don't try one in a game. Someone executing this kind of kick will fall to the ground on his back or side after making the kick. An inexperienced player trying this could well injure an arm, shoulder, neck, or head.

PICKUP GAMES Since soccer is a game that can be played almost anywhere, a group of players might decide to play on their own. Without supervision, on a rough field, and without the right shoes and protective equipment, injuries can happen more often.

These games can sometimes become wild kicking contests with feet connecting with shins more than with the ball. Uneven fields can cause ankle and leg injuries. And without supervision and a referee, tempers can erupt into fistfights. Know who you are playing before you start a pickup game. If you use the game to practice your skills and have fun, that's fine. Otherwise, you may just find yourself in a rough-and-tumble game with more than one person getting hurt.

BIKING AND SWIMMING

Biking and swimming are probably the two most widespread recreational activities in the country. National Safety Council statistics compiled in 1992 show more than 54.5 million Americans taking part in biking and more than 63 million hitting the water to go swimming. There are undoubtedly even more than that.

Many more injuries occur in biking than swimming. That doesn't mean safe swimming isn't important. Mistakes made in the water can immediately create a chance of a drowning. And that's about as bad an accident as anyone can have. So while biking and swimming might appear to be second nature to those who have been doing them almost all their lives, there are still precautions that should be taken to keep things on the safe side.

BIKING

A bicycle can serve many purposes. It can take you to a friend's house quickly, help you deliver papers and make some spending money, and take you a long distance much faster than if you walk. It can be the means to compete against others in a race, or it can take you up and down hills and over rough terrain. A bicycle can be used to express your athleticism through tricks and fancy maneuvers.

What you do with a bicycle depends on the type of bike you

have and what gives you the most enjoyment. City riding, racing, trick riding, and mountain biking are all different. So are the dangers they present. Riding in traffic and riding down a rocky hillside pose distinctly different dangers. So you must be aware of the safety precautions connected with each style of riding you do.

TYPES OF BICYCLES   The touring bike is lightweight with a small, hard seat and thin, hard tires. The handlebars are curved downward. These bikes don't have fenders and have caliper brakes on both wheels with the brake levers on the handlebars. The best touring bikes weigh barely twenty pounds and are designed for general and long-distance street riding. These bikes now have at least eighteen different gears.

The BMX (Bicycle Motocross) bike has thick, twenty-inch tires and a strong frame. There is also a smaller version with sixteen-inch tires for very young riders. BMX bikes use only one gear and have caliper brakes on both tires that are controlled by levers on the handlebars. A street version of the bike may come with coaster brakes, which are operated by the pedals.

These bikes are used for racing over rugged motocross courses with bumps, banked turns, and jumps. They are also used for all kinds of trick riding and jumping. BMX bikes are very rugged and can take a real beating.

Mountain bikes are the most recently developed style of bikes. Mountain biking has become a very popular sport in the 1990s. These bikes grew out of the BMX bikes, so riders could do more off-road riding. These bikes are very durable and lightweight. They have thick, rugged tires and very strong wheels. The handlebars are straight and the bike is equipped with powerful caliper brakes on both the front and rear wheels.

On the more expensive mountain bikes, the front forks have shock absorbers like those on a car. Mountain bikes have between fifteen and eighteen gears and are built for use on all kinds of off-road and rugged terrain, as well as for racing over that terrain.

KEEPING YOUR BIKE IN GOOD SHAPE Whether you have a regular touring bike, a BMX racer, or a mountain bike, you want to make sure that the bike is in good shape. Each bike, of course, is designed for a different type of riding. For your own safety, always have the right kind of bike for the kind of riding you want to do.

For example, never run a touring bike around a BMX racetrack or up and down a rocky trail. The bike isn't designed for that kind of pounding. And if the bike fails, you can get hurt. At the same time, a one-gear BMX is not made to climb steep hills or a sloped mountainside. Using a BMX bike for this kind of riding will make the rider tire and increase the chance for an accident or injury.

Once you have the bike you want, always be sure to keep it in tip-top condition. If your bike fails you at the wrong time, you may not be able to avoid an injury. Here is a basic checklist for keeping your bike ready to ride:

1. Check and tighten any loose bolts on the brake levers, gear-shift levers, stem, handlebar, and bar ends.
2. Check the welded joints on the bike frame for any signs of cracking. Rough riding can cause even the best frames to crack sooner or later.
3. Make sure the bottoms of your brake pads are even with the sides of the wheel rims. Learn how to adjust them. If the pads are worn, replace them.
4. Examine your tires for signs of wear. If the tread is low or the "knobbies" are worn, replace the tire. Also replace the tire if there are any cuts or tears in it. You don't want a blowout at the wrong time.
5. Look for any other signs of weakness, such as frayed brake cables, loose pedals, or broken spokes.

You don't have to be an expert mechanic to keep your bike in safe condition. But you do have to recognize warning signs of bicycle breakdown. There are many books you can read that will teach you more about your bike. Always take action when you think something is wrong. If you can't fix it, take it to someone who can. But make sure it is fixed before you ride in traffic, race on a rough course, or climb or descend a steep mountain.

Whatever kind of riding you plan to do, here are some basic safety rules you should keep in mind:

1. **Wear a helmet.** This is an absolute must for any kind of biking. Many states now make it a *law* for youngsters under a certain age to wear a helmet as soon as they get on a bike. A good helmet can prevent a serious head injury. Open-face helmets are fine for most forms of street riding. Full-face helmets, which cover not only the head but much of the face, are also available and may be preferable for racing or for riding over rough terrain.

2. **Think about clothing.** In summer, the temptation is often to ride wearing just shorts and a T-shirt. That leaves your hands, arms, elbows, knees, and legs open for cuts, bruises, and a bad scrape known as "road rash." If you don't want to wear long pants and long sleeves, you might consider knee and elbow pads, which will give you some protection if you fall or slip. Gloves and wrist guards are also available.

3. **Plan ahead for long trips.** If you are with a group taking a long "bike hike" that will keep you out for a good part of the day, there are several things to keep in mind. Plan ahead. Know where you are going and where you can find shelter. Also get a weather report and don't go if severe weather is predicted. Remember that it can be much warmer at noon than at six o'clock in the evening. If the weather cools in late afternoon, bring along extra clothing. And take some sunscreen with you.

Always bring water, to prevent dehydration. In addition, the water can also be used if someone falls and gets cut and the cut needs to be cleaned. For long trips, someone in the group should carry a basic first-aid kit, and everyone should carry identification in case of an accident.

You should also have a basic repair kit, including a spare inner tube, and an air pump. All touring bikes can be fitted with luggage racks and other means to carry extra gear.

4. **Observe the rules of the road.** All bikers must know the traffic laws because they must observe them. That means obeying all stop signs and traffic signals. Ride only on the right side of the road as near the curb or shoulder as possible. You should be riding with the traffic. Never ride facing traffic and don't weave in and out of traffic. Be aware that the door of a parked car may open suddenly. Always ride single file. Never ride on sidewalks and always respect pedestrians. Remember—the pedestrian has the right of way.

5. **Use hand signals.** Hand signals let the traffic around you know your intentions. A right turn is indicated by holding the left arm straight up at the elbow. A left turn is indicated by holding the left arm straight out. Stopping or slowing down is indicated by holding the left arm straight down at the elbow. Always use these basic signals when riding in traffic. If you are riding where there are designated bike lanes, be careful when entering and leaving the lanes. Use your hand signals. And even though you are in a bike lane, stay alert for other vehicles that don't belong there.

6. **Use lights at night.** Always have your bike equipped for night riding. Use reflectors on the pedals and wheels. There are light kits available to give you both a white front light and red rear light. It will also help to wear reflective clothing or reflective tape on your clothing. You want to be sure you can see and that others can see you.

STREET RIDING RULES One of the biggest dangers bikers face on the streets is, obviously, automobiles. The more traffic, the greater the danger. A lonely country road is certainly not as dangerous as a busy city street with cars, trucks, buses, taxicabs, people, and other bikes. Traveling just one block under those conditions can be more dangerous than a fifty-mile bike hike in the country.

Here are some things you *shouldn't* do when riding your bike on the street:

1. Don't make sudden turns or stops without warning.
2. Never horse around or race someone else in heavy traffic.
3. Don't try to get a free ride by grabbing onto the back of a truck or bus. This can lead to a bad fall or fling you into a line of traffic. You also can slip under the wheels of the vehicle that's towing you.
4. Don't carry another person on your bike. This will make steering and balance difficult and can block your vision.
5. Don't carry anything extra in your arms. Use a basket or luggage rack.
6. Keep two hands on the handlebars. You may be able to ride with no hands, but you won't be able to react to an emergency. Save "no hands" and other tricks for when you aren't in traffic.

BMX AND MOUNTAIN BIKE RACING   When you race over a BMX course you are competing directly against other riders. When you try to conquer rugged terrain on a mountain bike you are competing against the environment. And when you race a mountain bike, you might be going up against the clock and the mountain. But racing is racing, and it always involves an element of risk and danger.

The first rule of racing is simple. *Don't do it unless you have the skills for it.* If you aren't already an expert rider, don't tackle competitive racing. If your skill as a rider isn't as good as your competitors', you not only won't win, but you might get hurt.

What skills do you need? For BMX racing you have to know how to take jumps, ride around banked and flat turns, and keep

*BMX racers need to master a variety of skills
before entering into competition.*

your speed and balance over a series of bumps called whoop-de-doos. You should practice these skills before trying them with six or seven other riders on the track.

Mountain bikers must ride on narrow trails, take jumps, go over rocks, logs, and any other debris that might be on the trail. The rider must learn how to take turns and also how to brake on all kinds of surfaces, from soft sand to rocky ground.

Everyone who rides a bicycle is going to fall at some time or another. Some wipeouts are worse than others. But you can learn how to relax and roll with the fall to minimize injury. Falls during a BMX or mountain bike race can be worse than when you're simply riding for pleasure. That's why you should wear more protective gear (knee and elbow pads, gloves) when you race.

SWIMMING

Millions of people enjoy swimming each year. It's one of the most widespread and popular recreational activities in the world. Whether in a smooth lake, the cold choppy ocean, a warm swimming pool, or an old, muddy swimming hole, kids of all ages love the water once they learn to swim. And compared to other sports, injuries suffered while swimming are relatively few.

Surprisingly, people are not natural swimmers. Throw a nonswimmer into the water and she will not suddenly do the crawl or the breaststroke. More than likely, she will panic, struggle, and possibly drown.

Most people today swim for fun. Others like to race. But whether you are racing toward the Olympics or just swimming to cool off and get some exercise, there are certain rules of safety that should always be followed.

EVERYONE SHOULD LEARN TO SWIM   If possible, everyone should learn to swim. You don't want to find yourself in deep water without knowing how to stay afloat. Swimming is an easy skill for most people to learn. Rule number one is not to fear the water. That's why it's possible to teach infants to swim even before they walk. They haven't developed a fear of going under the water. Sometimes, the longer you wait to learn to swim, the more fear you build up, and learning becomes harder. So learn to swim as soon as possible.

Without fear of the water, you can probably learn from a good swimmer—a friend, parent, guardian, or relative. Or you can learn from a qualified instructor who is trained to help people overcome their fear. Once you learn to swim, you'll never forget. With practice and time in the water, you will become a stronger swimmer.

Even strong swimmers need to be aware of some basic rules of swimming safety. If you follow these rules, you can lessen your chances of having a water-related accident.

KNOW WHERE YOU ARE SWIMMING   One of the primary rules of swimming safety is to pay attention to where you are swimming. If you are in a designated swimming area at a lake, a pool, or even the ocean, there will probably be lifeguards on hand to watch you and everyone else. They won't let you swim too far from shore or in out-of-bounds areas. Chances are if you get into trouble, they will be right on the spot to help you.

If you are swimming in the ocean, you must be aware of tides and currents. If the currents are very strong, the lifeguards may not let you go into the water. Always obey their instructions. Never look for a place down the beach that might not be patrolled and swim there. Currents can sometimes carry even a strong swimmer out to sea.

Ocean beaches can also have high waves crashing in on the shore. Some high waves are fun. But really high waves can be dangerous. If you're not prepared, they can stun you and pull you underwater. They can also create what is called an undertow. You might be standing in ankle-deep water. But after a

RIPTIDES

In a large body of water, such as oceans, currents can be stronger and swifter than in smaller lakes and inlets. And every once in a while the tide can become downright dangerous. When conditions are right, a riptide can occur. A riptide is often strong enough to carry even excellent swimmers out to sea.

Riptides start with large waves, or breakers, crashing onto the beach. These breakers cast huge amounts of water up onto the sand. This water must return to the sea. The returning currents can create an undertow that can knock an adult off her feet.

When water cast up on the beach at one place finds its way back to the sea at another place, this creates rip currents, or a riptide. These strong currents flow away from the shore at certain points with enough strength to prevent even a good swimmer from getting to the shore.

If you are ever caught in a riptide while swimming, the trick is not to try to swim straight to shore. If you are in the riptide, you might not make it. Instead, swim parallel to the shoreline for a short distance. This should take you out of the riptide and allow you to then swim safely straight in to shore.

wave hits, there is suddenly water over your knees running rapidly back out to sea. Small children can be dragged under by this kind of undertow. So with high waves you always have to be extra careful.

Lakes and swimming holes can present other problems,

especially if they are not patrolled. There is a good chance of sharp objects being on the bottom—shells, jagged rocks, possibly even broken glass. If you are in bare feet and walking into unknown water, tread very lightly. You may get a severe cut and not have any first aid nearby. That can make it worse.

DON'T JUMP OR DIVE INTO UNKNOWN WATER Jumping into the water is fun; diving into the water (headfirst) is a skill. Both can be dangerous for several reasons. If you are going to jump or dive into a crowded pool, make sure the area below you is clear. If you land on another swimmer, both of you might get injured.

Never dive-bomb someone else, either in a pool or off a float. Jumping in right alongside and splashing someone may scare that person. That, in itself, isn't a smart idea. If you misjudge your jump and collide with the person, you're risking injury to both of you. That kind of horsing around isn't allowed in supervised swimming areas, and it shouldn't be done in unsupervised areas, either.

Diving into unknown waters poses a special kind of danger. Here is an essential rule that should never be forgotten: *if you don't know how deep the water is, DON'T DIVE!* If you dive into shallow water, you can easily suffer a head or neck injury with devastating results. Severe neck injuries can cause paralysis or death. Don't risk your life for a minute of fun.

It isn't a good idea to jump into unknown water, either, especially from a high takeoff point. It might seem cool to leap off a high wall and sail down twenty-five or thirty feet into the water. But there may be hidden dangers beneath the surface, and a serious injury could result.

CLOWNING AROUND You can have all kinds of fun around the water without playing practical jokes that may result in injury. A common prank is to push or throw someone into the water. Sometimes two people will pick up a third and swing-throw that

*Always take the time to look before you leap.
Jumping or diving into unknown waters can easily
cause devastating injuries.*

person into the water, accompanied by great laughter.

This, however, isn't funny. Someone who doesn't want to be thrown into the water shouldn't be thrown in. That person might not know how to swim. Or she might not be feeling well. Or she might not have a change of clothes. By throwing this person into the water, you might scare her so badly that she will have to be rescued. You may cause her to come down with an illness. Or you may injure her.

One danger of throwing or pushing someone into a pool or into a lake from a float is that she can strike her head or another part of her body on the side of the pool or float. That can result in a serious injury. In addition, if there is someone in the water, the person being thrown in can land on her, resulting in another injury.

MORE RULES FOR SAFE SWIMMING Here are a few more basic rules every swimmer needs to observe:

1. **Never swim alone.** Make sure you have at least one buddy with you whenever you swim.
2. **Know the currents.** The ocean isn't the only body of water with potentially tricky currents—rivers and streams can be dangerous, too. Don't ever make the mistake of underestimating the water or overestimating your ability to swim in it.
3. **Beware of muscle cramps.** For years, mothers have been telling their children not to go into the water for an hour after eating. A full stomach and strenuous swimming in cold water can cause severe stomach cramps. Stomach cramps can be extremely dangerous because they can cause a swimmer to double over in the water. If you get a stomach cramp, try to relax, keep your head above water, and call for help. If you get a foot or leg cramp, float on your back and try to massage the cramped muscle. Relax and swim slowly toward shore using a different stroke than the one you were doing. The cramp should work itself out.

SUNBURN AND SUNSCREEN

There was a time, not so long ago, when many people intentionally baked in the sun, trying to get as much of a suntan as they could. People thought they looked better with a tan. It has only been in recent years that solid evidence has been found to prove that prolonged exposure to sunlight can be bad for your health.

Among the forms of energy radiating from the sun are ultraviolet rays. Some of these rays are blocked from reaching the earth by the atmosphere. But scientific evidence has shown that the ozone layer in the atmosphere, the layer that protects against ultraviolet rays, is thinning. More of these rays are now reaching the earth, not only causing skin to tan and burn, but causing skin cancer as well.

People with very light, fair skin are the most susceptible. But everyone is now advised to keep exposure to the sun to a minimum. If you are going to be out in the sun, at the beach or on the water, it is suggested that you use a good waterproof sunblock to protect your skin.

You should apply a sunblock about thirty minutes before going out, even on an overcast day. Reapply it after swimming or after perspiring heavily.

Not only is a bad sunburn painful, but it can take three to six months for your skin to return to normal. The top or burned layer will peel off and the newly exposed skin is more sensitive and will burn faster than ever.

4. **Watch out for sunburn.** Exposure to the sun goes hand-in-hand with a day at the beach or at poolside. Too much sun can be dangerous. Not only can it dry the skin, it can make it vulnerable to skin cancer. Since water reflects the sun, you can even get a bad sunburn while you are swimming.

   Never just bask in the sun. When you aren't in the water wear a brimmed cap and a T-shirt. It's also a good idea to use a sunblock on exposed areas of your body, even when you go into the water.

5. **Learn CPR.** Whenever people are swimming, there is a possibility that someone may drown. That's a sobering thought. Today, all lifeguards must know cardiopulmonary resuscitation (CPR). CPR can get a drowning victim breathing again and keep her breathing until the paramedics arrive. Courses in CPR are given at local hospitals, fire departments, first-aid squads, and other locations. If you do a lot of swimming and spend a lot of time around the water, it may be a good idea to learn CPR. It isn't difficult and might enable you to save a life. More details on CPR are given in chapter 6.

STREET SPORTS

In both cities and rural areas, there are always a number of popular street activities that become widespread among youngsters. These are recreational activities that aren't classified as team sports. Nor are they organized. Yet these are activities that take athleticism and skill. And because they are developed to a high level, they contain an element of risk and the potential for serious injury.

Two of the most popular and controversial street activities of the mid-1990s are in-line skating and skateboarding. Both sports have become so popular that they have become organized to some degree. In-line skaters can now join roller-hockey leagues or compete in races. Skateboarders compete in the half-pipe, doing tricks as they skate up and down parallel ramps, and in some places have designated areas set up where they can practice tricks and enjoy the thrill of special kinds of riding.

But for our purpose, we will stick to the street version of these sports. They are, for the most part, unsupervised. And they are practiced by kids who become very skilled, have little fear, and try new things at high speed without a great deal of protection. And that's when injuries can occur.

IN-LINE SKATING

In-line skating is perhaps the fastest-growing sport or recreational activity in the United States. Unlike traditional roller

*Skating parks are great places for in-line
skaters to show off their skills.*

skates, with two wheels on the front and back of the skate, in-line skates have a single row of four wheels in the middle of the skate. They are almost like ice skates with wheels and allow the skater tremendous speed and movement.

There is no doubt that in-line skating is a great activity for people of all ages. It's fun, exciting, healthful, and, as desired, competitive. But with more and more skaters taking to the rinks, roads, sidewalks, and trails every year, the number of injuries from this sport have increased dramatically.

The National Safety Council logged 10,800 in-line skating injuries in 1992. By 1993, the number had risen to 37,000. Then in 1994 it jumped to 76,000. Estimates for 1995 predicted that more than 105,000 in-line skaters would be treated at hospital emergency rooms for injuries received while skating. As more people put on the single-line wheeled blades every year, the number of injuries increases accordingly.

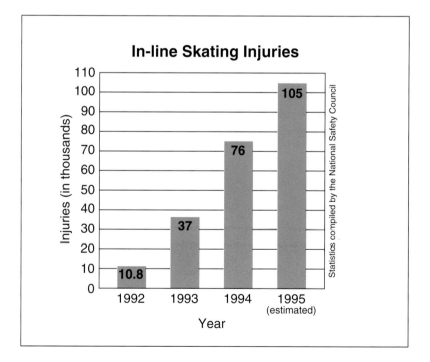

A VERSATILE ACTIVITY   There is much more to in-line skating than just straight-ahead movement. The blades are very versatile. Street skaters love to jump over obstacles and maneuver in and out of tight places. Those who can find skating parks can learn how to ride ramps and even do the same kind of half-pipe tricks that snowboarders and skateboarders do. There are organized races, downhill slalom courses, and roller-hockey leagues springing up everywhere.

Skiers use in-line skates to practice their slalom races where there is no snow available. Ice-hockey players can work on their skills by using in-line skates. Speed skaters can stay in condition with in-line skates without having to find a suitable ice rink. This is called cross training and has brought many more fine athletes to in-line skating.

But the versatility of in-line skates has also created problems. Unfortunately, those who don't have access to a skating park or don't want to play roller hockey often find themselves taking to the streets looking for cool places to skate. That's where much of the trouble begins. Skateboarding, for instance, has always thrived on something of an "outlaw" image and attitude. Some of that has come over to in-line skating, as well.

Part of that image is to ignore the rules and just do your own thing. But if you ignore the rules, you might be setting yourself up for a serious injury.

AN AVOIDABLE TRAGEDY   In the spring of 1995, there was a story in the New York City newspapers that shocked a lot of people. Angier Biddle Duke, a seventy-nine-year-old millionaire and former United States diplomat, was killed when he stumbled into an oncoming car while on in-line skates and struck his head on the windshield.

The story was shocking for a number of reasons. For openers, here was a rather famous seventy-nine-year-old man on in-line skates in the middle of New York City. However, from all accounts, Mr. Duke was very hearty and very fit for his age. He used in-line skates frequently and enjoyed getting around on them. But when the entire story was told, it seemed that Mr. Duke had apparently chosen to ignore three important safety rules of in-line skating.

For starters, he should not have been skating near traffic, where one faltering step could cause him to move into the path of an oncoming vehicle. Second, he was wearing headphones. Loud music playing through headphones can cause you to miss the sound of an oncoming car or someone yelling at you to watch out. And, most important, Angier Biddle Duke was not wearing a helmet. That alone might have saved his life, since he died from a head injury.

From all accounts, Mr. Duke's age had very little to do with the accident. A short time later, two twelve-year-old boys were killed in separate accidents, also in New York City. Both were on in-line skates and skating in traffic. Both were killed by hit-and-run drivers. There are countless other similar examples. They all point out the need for extreme care and safety when using in-line skates.

LEARN THE BASIC SKILLS Anytime you are riding on wheels you must have complete control to be safe. You wouldn't ride a bike that had no brakes. Nor would you want to drive a car that didn't have a steering wheel. It's the same with in-line skates. You've got to start slowly and learn the skills that will allow you to skate under control. Unfortunately, many new skaters don't want to start slowly.

"Your average in-line skater really tends to want to push it," said Bruce Jackson, a top skater for years, during an interview. "That's one thing about an in-line skater. It's so much fun that you want to do more and more and more of it. I've seen that time and again just being around bladers and teaching so many people."

Jackson went on to say that beginners must learn all the techniques of skating properly, one step at a time. That means becoming comfortable on the skates and learning to move smoothly. Being able to turn left and right with equal ease is also necessary. Perhaps most important of all is learning how to stop.

In-line skates are equipped with a heel brake that takes getting used to. There are other stopping techniques as well. Learn them from a qualified skater and practice. Once you begin skating with some speed, you must be able to keep your balance while turning quickly and stopping as quickly as you can. Only then will you be ready for advanced kinds of skating.

THE PITFALLS Here's a quick list of some basic pitfalls that all bladers may encounter at one time or another and ways to deal with them:

1. **Falls.** Every in-line skater is going to fall at some time. In fact, doctors have said the major risk bladers face is injury to the wrists, since it's a natural reaction to reach out with the hands to break a fall. All bladers should learn to relax while falling, and try to go to the knees and roll. Turn right or left as you fall. Don't go straight down.

2. **Skating down hills.** Many skaters aren't ready for what happens on a hill. There is a sudden increase in speed that can take you by surprise. The faster you go, the harder it is to stop—wipeout city! So stay away from medium to steep hills until you are an absolute expert at stopping and changing direction.

3. **Slick surfaces.** Watch where you skate. If the skating surface is covered with oil, water, or sand, you might find yourself in trouble. The same goes for ice and snow. All can cause a slip or fall. The best thing to do is to skate across any slick surface slowly and in a straight line. Don't try to accelerate or turn. It's too slippery. Cracks and ruts in the pavement can also be a problem. While

they are not slick surfaces, they can snag a wheel and trip you.

4. **Traffic and pedestrians.** This one is a no-brainer. Avoid skating in areas of heavy vehicular traffic. If you find yourself on a road with light traffic, be extra careful and follow all traffic regulations. Skaters have also had problems on sidewalks. Always yield to pedestrians. No skater wants a high-speed collision with a pedestrian. That can result in injury for both of you.

5. **Local regulations.** There are often regulations regarding where in-line skaters can and cannot skate. Make sure you don't skate in restricted areas.

6. **Poor fitness.** As with any sport or physical activity, the better shape you are in, the better you will perform. If you are not in good physical condition you will tire easily, and the odds for a wipeout and injury will increase. So get in shape and stay there if you are going to skate.

WEAR THE RIGHT STUFF   In-line skating almost demands protective clothing as a prerequisite for safety. If you skate often you will fall, you will go down hills, and you will hit high speeds. And if you skate often, especially with friends, you will try new things, new challenges, and take some risks. Knowing this, it would be foolish not to protect yourself as much as possible.

Never, never skate without a good helmet. Some cities and states are now making it mandatory for skaters under a certain age to wear helmets, just as bicycle riders must. That's a clear indication of how concerned people are about the potential for injury in this sport.

While the helmet is the most important piece of a skater's gear, it isn't the only protection available. Skaters should always wear knee and elbow pads. Another essential piece of equipment is wrist guards. Some wrist guards have plastic inserts that help stabilize the wrist if it is used to break a fall, preventing or lessening sprains and breaks. There are also fingerless, padded skating gloves that protect the palms of the hands, which are also often used to break falls.

If you must skate during twilight or after dark, it is a good idea to wear reflective clothing or reflective tape on your clothing. Reflective tape enables drivers of approaching autos to see you as soon as you are in range of their headlights. However, skating after dark always presents a greater risk. Try to stay off your skates at night.

As for the skates, there are now many different brands on the market. Choose the best skates you can afford, because the better the construction, the more stability they will provide for your foot and ankle during rugged use. Make sure that the skates fit you properly. Skates that are too loose or too tight can cause you problems. Remember to check your wheels and brakes, and replace them when necessary.

SKATEBOARDING

Many of the safety rules for in-line skating also apply to skateboarding. Skateboarding remains a popular street activity among kids in many areas. There was a time when the sport was more organized. There were slalom and downhill races (similar to those in skiing), half-pipe riding, as well as flatland freestyle contests, where riders did tricks on their boards while skating on a flat surface or rink. But many of those activities have fallen by the wayside. Today, street-style skateboarding is the most popular form of the sport.

Unfortunately, street-style skateboarding also has a kind of outlaw image. In urban areas, pedestrians and store owners consider the boards noisy and dangerous. And there are skateboarders who flaunt the rules. They seem to feel that any obstacle in their path is fair game.

This image has detracted from what has always been a sport that takes a great deal of daring and skill. Half-pipe riders are

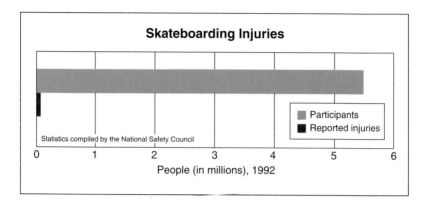

Skateboarding Injuries

Participants
Reported injuries

Statistics compiled by the National Safety Council

0 1 2 3 4 5 6

People (in millions), 1992

amazing as they go up and down ramps, doing spins, flips, and handstands, all while staying on their boards. For street-stylers, there is a great deal of jumping and sliding over obstacles, which also takes practice and skill. But where daring and skill are present, there is also the potential for injury.

The last set of figures compiled by the National Safety Council in 1992 showed some 5.5 million skateboarders in the United States with 44,068 injuries treated in hospital emergency rooms. There were undoubtedly many more bumps and bruises that were not reported.

STREET-STYLE SKATEBOARDING   What, exactly, is meant by street-style skateboarding?

"When it started it was kind of goofy," explained Rodney Mullin, who was a professional skateboarding champion. In an interview he explained that "Guys began launching themselves against obstacles like walls and benches. But gradually it became more technical. A lot of street guys can do all the old competitive freestyle tricks, and now they have tricks of their own."

Those tricks include a whole lot of jumps, called ollies. Street-riders will jump up onto curbs or ollie onto a handrail. Then they slide down the rail on the board. This is a dangerous maneuver that can lead to a bad fall.

Skateboarders often slide down handrails on their boards.
Only the best skaters can do an ollie without falling.

Skaters sometimes ollie up onto a bench and ride the corner on their boards. There are also special spins and jumps when the rider leaves a moving board and then returns to it. This takes timing and skill, with the potential for a fall always there.

Street-stylers often look at any obstacle as a challenge. Can I jump it? Can I ollie on and ollie off? For that reason, many people resent skateboarders, and the authorities often have to ban them from certain areas. But with some care and imagination, skateboarding can still be an exciting activity.

PROTECT YOUR BODY   In some ways, skateboarding is similar to in-line skating. The sport involves wheels and speed. A rider can fall or really wipe out. That makes certain kinds of protective gear necessary. Unfortunately, part of the skateboarding outlaw image says it isn't cool to wear protective gear.

Gear for skateboarders isn't fancy. In fact, it's nearly identical to that of in-line skaters—helmet, knee guards, elbow pads, gloves, and wrist guards. Since a lot of skateboarding is done in warm-weather areas, boarders sometimes feel it's a hassle to wear protective gear. That's a mistake. Think about what you do on the board—jump, ollie, spin, turn, ride rails. You're going to slip and you're going to fall. Helmets and pads could prevent a serious injury.

Boarders have their own lingo for injuries. There's a "wrist slam," "chin skin," and "hipper." One of the most painful injuries is called a "swellbow," in which the sac protecting the elbow fills with fluid after repeated bangs and knocks.

DO'S AND DON'TS   Here is a quick checklist of things even skilled skateboarders need to pay attention to:

1. **Hone your skills.** Make sure you have the basic skills before you try advanced tricks. Learn to move, turn, and stop. Know how to get off the board quickly if trouble looms.

2. **Find a good place to skate.** Since many places are off-limits to skateboarders, you should look for a designated place to skate and practice. It may be a playground or a park. If there are no good places around, you and your friends should speak to your parents or guardians. They might be able to help find or create a place to skateboard safely. Never build your own ramps or jumps unless you are guided by an expert. Otherwise, this will only increase the chances that you'll get hurt.

3. **Obey traffic rules.** If you are skating on the street you must obey all traffic signs, signals, and rules. Use common sense around traffic. Avoid it when you can. One wrong move and a serious injury might result.

4. **Never skate at night.** Bright, reflective clothing or tape can help to make you more visible. But there are still pitfalls. You can't always see the skating surface and might not be able to judge distance well. You may also be blinded by oncoming headlights, even if you're on the sidewalk. To be on the safe side, it's better to be off the board after dark.

5. **Never hitch a ride.** Sometimes boarders hitch a quick ride by grabbing onto a passing car or truck. It can be a quick ride to the hospital if your luck runs out, even if you are wearing protective gear. So just don't do it.

6. **Know how to fall.** Everyone falls at some time. With many street-style maneuvers, a skater can simply hop off the board in the nick of time. If you feel yourself falling at high speed or while trying a midair maneuver, relax your body, then twist and roll with the fall. Try to distribute the impact to as much of the body as possible. Don't try to break your fall with just your arms.

7. **Learn from the best.** No skateboarder knows everything. To improve your skills, watch the good boarders in action. Ask questions. Let a top boarder watch your technique and give you advice.

8. **Don't take dares.** A challenge to learn a new trick or maneuver is one thing. A foolish, risk-taking dare is another. Don't be goaded

into trying something too difficult or something dangerous on your board. Use common sense whenever you're on your board.

STREET GAMES

Street games are really too numerous to mention one by one. That's because kids make up new ones every day. There are old standbys like tag, red light, hide-and-seek, and stickball. Whatever the game, the basic rules of safety are the same: don't take any unnecessary chances. Don't be goaded into rough play. Don't play in heavy traffic.

The object of any game, sport, or recreational activity is fun. Don't spoil things for yourself or for anyone else by taking your fun to the edge.

HIKING

Hiking is an activity that can be enjoyed by people of all ages. Sometimes it's simply family fun. Other times it is an organized activity through a group such as the Boy Scouts. Some hikers go into completely foreign territory, traveling from a big city to walk in the woods. Others go into familiar territory time and time again.

The thing that all hikers share is an element of risk and danger. Some like hiking into unexplored and unfamiliar territory. Others are simply novices not quite prepared to take on the elements that await them. Each must be aware of the dangers that can come along during both short and long hikes.

INTO THE COUNTRY

If someone from the city goes hiking or backpacking, it's usually an organized and supervised activity. The hikers are told what to bring and the organizers take care of the rest. Every possible measure is taken to ensure the safety of the hikers.

But kids in rural, wooded, or mountainous regions often take off on their own. Many have grown up around the area and feel at home there. Sometimes they will go out hiking without any prior planning. Because they are familiar with the area, they tend to take chances and challenge themselves to try new and perhaps even dangerous things. That's when fun can turn into tragedy.

Whenever you go out into a wooded or mountainous area, there are things you must consider. You must know the direction in which you are going. Don't just wander aimlessly. If you plan to hike a number of miles, then return to your starting point, make sure you know how to return. You can travel on marked trails or use a compass to travel in a certain direction both going and returning. You can also sight natural landmarks in the distance, such as a high tree or mountaintop, and hike in their direction. Remember, you'll also need a landmark to direct your return trip!

DRESS FOR SUCCESS   The tips here are not for hikers and backpackers who plan to be out several days or more and who are going to be setting up a campsite. Serious hiking and camping is really a separate category. The advice given here is for kids who just decide to have some fun for a few hours in the woods or hills.

Suppose, for instance, you and your friend are shooting hoops in the driveway. After a while, you become bored and look for something else to do. Your friend says he knows a place where you can climb some rocks about a mile or two away. Both of you just take off and go.

Since it's a hot summer day, you're wearing shorts, a T-shirt, and your basketball shoes. That's it. Right away, you may be headed for trouble. Your clothing is totally inadequate for what you are about to do.

For openers, walking or hiking shoes give more protection than basketball shoes or sneakers. Air Jordans may be great when you take a jump shot, but they won't give you that much stability on a rocky trail. Next, you've got to get rid of the shorts. Blue jeans or other sturdy pants are better. There are several reasons for this.

In shorts, your legs can be scraped and bruised by thick

brush and rocks. If you fall, you will have little protection from injury. In addition, without long pants you will be more susceptible to insect bites, poison ivy, and possibly snake bites. In certain parts of the country, you need to be aware of the tiny deer tick that can cause Lyme disease. There is less chance of this tick attaching itself to you if you wear long pants. For added protection, you can tuck the bottoms of your pants legs into your socks.

A long-sleeved shirt can help protect you, too. But if it is hot you can probably cheat a little here. Still, a heavier shirt will protect you more than a thin T-shirt. Add a hat, too. A hat will shade you from the sun and keep low-hanging branches and insects out of your hair and face.

IT'S DIFFERENT IN WINTER   The above scenario was for a hot summer day. If you are in a seasonal climate, you would dress according to the weather before leaving on your hike. In colder weather, always wear several layers of clothing and a warm hat. In fall and spring, keep in mind that the temperature can drop quite rapidly once the sun goes down.

Always remember the time of year and know how long you plan to stay out before you take off on a hike.

DON'T TAKE RISKS FAR FROM HOME   It's one thing if you get hurt in your own backyard or at school or at the local park. You can almost always get help immediately. But if you go off hiking and get hurt, help may be miles away. There will not be a telephone nearby. No one will hear your shouts for help. This is the main reason why you should never hike alone. But even if you are with a buddy, that person will have to go for help. And that can take time.

Here are some basic tips for those who decide to venture into the great outdoors for a few hours of fun:

1. **Stay on the trail.** If you are on a trail, stay on it. That makes getting back easy. If you decide to leave the trail, don't go far and always look for a landmark that will take you right back to the trail. If you're off the trail and get careless, it's easy to lose your way. In addition, once you leave the trail, the terrain can become steep or dangerous in some other way, and you simply won't be prepared for it.

2. **Let someone know where you are going.** Don't ever take off without telling someone—a friend, a parent or guardian—where you are going. That way, if you become lost and people have to search for you, they will have a good idea of where to start.

3. **If you get lost.** Don't panic. That's rule number one. Don't scurry off in one direction, then another. Sit down and think. Maybe you can reach high ground and spot a landmark. If you climb a tree hoping to spot a landmark, make sure it's a tree you can climb down from easily. If you want to try and find your way, make sure you can get back to the place where you first realized that you were lost. That way, even if you don't find your way out, you won't have made your situation any worse than it already is. If all else fails, try to make a shelter, stay warm, and wait for someone to find you.

4. **Walk, don't run.** Falls are always a danger on a rough trail. Hiking is just what it says. Don't run. There are too many obstacles—fallen logs, rocks, low-hanging branches, or a sudden downhill—on a trail. If you horse around and begin running or racing with a friend, you might easily take a bad fall.

5. **Amateurs shouldn't climb rocks.** Rock climbing is a sport that takes skill, practice, and special equipment. Yet kids often have the urge to climb something, and if you come across a rocky slope, you might decide to try climbing it. This can result in a serious accident. If you fall while climbing, you can easily break a bone or suffer a head injury. The rule works both ways, incidentally. Don't try to climb up; and don't try to climb down. You can get injured either way.

No one should ever hike alone. Bringing a map of the area you'll be hiking in is a good idea, too.

ROCK CLIMBING

If you climb, you can fall. If you fall, you can get seriously hurt. So if you like to climb, or decide to take up a challenge while hiking, you should make it your business to learn how to climb. The best way is to get some tips from an expert, someone who thinks about safety first.

There are different types of climbing. We are not talking about major mountains, but just a rocky slope of varying degrees of steepness. Rock climbers today generally prefer to wear nonrestrictive, lightweight clothing so they can move freely. Of course, you shouldn't climb a dangerous slope alone. Always have one or more other climbers with you.

The most basic piece of equipment to have is a strong, nylon rope. It can literally become a lifeline between you and other climbers. You should be in fine physical condition with strong hands, arms, and legs.

Climbers can practice on man-made climbing walls that are now located in many sports centers. They are vertical walls with protruding grips you can hang on to and notches for your feet. But it still takes strength and skill to scale one of these walls. Climbers are aided by a rope and attached to a safety harness, so they will not get hurt if they fall.

Learning to climb

6. Watch the weather. Sudden changes in the weather have caught even experienced hikers by surprise. But they are usually prepared with equipment that will help them cope. You may not be. A rainstorm can leave you soaked and cold. A thunderstorm with high winds and lightning can be even more dangerous. Sudden temperature drops can also catch you unaware. A snow squall can drop several inches of snow in an hour or less. And if you spend time in an open area, the sun can give you a nasty burn. So don't stay out too long. Try to get a weather report before you leave. When the weather is iffy, don't go. An unexpected change in the weather can really spoil a good time.

Kids have had adventurous spirits since long before the days of Huck Finn and Tom Sawyer. But reality is not a novel. If you take off for an adventure in the woods or in the hills, be careful not to bite off more than you can chew.

WEATHER DANGERS

Changes in the weather have been mentioned a number of times in this book. Sure, you can get sunburned, drenched, or snowed on. But all you need to do is care for the sunburn, dry out, or warm up and take a hot shower. You are usually not affected very seriously.

There are, however, several very serious problems that can be a direct result of ignoring the weather around you. Let's take a brief look at each one.

HEAT EXHAUSTION

There is a difference between heat exhaustion and heatstroke. Heat exhaustion is rarely a critical condition, but the situation still must be corrected quickly. Heat exhaustion is caused by a lengthy exposure to high temperatures, with or without direct sunlight. The situation can be made worse by high humidity.

What are the symptoms to watch for? Painful muscle spasms in the legs and abdomen are the first sign that the body is having trouble dealing with heat. Weakness, dizziness, and headache may also occur. The skin will be cold and clammy, and the victim may feel nauseous. He may also begin sweating freely. This is called a cold sweat. The victim is losing too much water and also suffering loss of salt from the body.

If you begin to feel this way while exercising, do the following things quickly:

1. Get to the coolest possible place: an air-conditioned room, store, or mall. If there is no air-conditioning available, try to find a fan; a fan will cool you by causing perspiration to evaporate.
2. Lie down and loosen any tight or restrictive clothing.
3. Drink liquids in small amounts. Vomiting up the liquid is an indication that your condition is dangerous. If this happens, you need an ambulance right away.
4. Despite the salt loss, do not take salt tablets or eat salty snacks. Instead try to get an electrolyte drink such as Gatorade, which will replace the sodium (salt is sodium chloride) you have lost.
5. Do not take any medication such as aspirin or anything to take away nausea.
6. If you begin feeling better, don't return to the heat or go out into the sun. You may have a relapse. Just call it quits for that day.

Heat exhaustion can often be prevented by drinking a lot of fluids before you go out and then during the time you are in the heat. When you continue to play and sweat, and don't replace the fluid you've lost, you can get into trouble.

HEATSTROKE

The difference between heat exhaustion and heatstroke is simple. Heatstroke can kill you. Heatstroke, sometimes called sunstroke, is caused by exposure to very high temperatures and is usually accompanied by physical exertion. One symptom that sets heatstroke apart from heat exhaustion is that the victim's body temperature rises to dangerously high levels.

Symptoms appear quickly. The victim may suddenly pass out. His skin will be hot, dry, and red. When he awakens, he may have a weak and rapid pulse and shallow breathing. He may also go into convulsions, or be confused or disoriented. And he won't be sweating at all. That's the real telltale sign of heatstroke. Remember, heat exhaustion victims go into a profuse cold sweat.

One of the best ways to prevent heat exhaustion is to drink plenty of fluids—both before and during exercise—when temperatures are high.

The victim's sudden, high temperature can be fatal in heat-stroke cases. Death can occur quickly, so there is no time to waste. Here's what to do:

1. Call for professional help. Waste no time in calling for an ambulance or getting someone to take the victim to the nearest hospital.
2. While waiting for help to arrive, try to get the victim into an air-conditioned area. Remove most of the victim's clothing. Splash him with cold water. This is better than immersing the victim in a tub or pool since the water will evaporate on the skin and more quickly reduce the victim's body temperature.
3. If ice is available, use ice packs to cool the victim's body. Placing ice packs in the victim's armpits, behind the neck, and in the groin area can help cool him faster. Towels soaked in cold water are another option. You are trying to get the victim's temperature down before help arrives.
4. Do not give any medication.
5. If the victim regains consciousness and says he is fine, don't listen. A victim of heatstroke must be hospitalized, even if he appears to have recovered.

While infants and older people are at greater risk, heat-stroke can happen to anyone under the right conditions. If you are exerting yourself in extreme heat, drink plenty of fluids (especially electrolyte drinks like Gatorade) and take periodic rest periods. If you feel any symptoms of either heat exhaustion or heatstroke, stop what you are doing *immediately* and go somewhere to cool down.

HYPOTHERMIA

Now we go from hot to cold. Hypothermia is a dangerous drop in body temperature. The body should have an internal temperature of about 98.6°F. Below 92°F, cardiac arrest can occur. It's that simple. Lose body heat and you are in trouble. If you

CALL 9-1-1

Everyone should know the best and fastest way to get help in the event of an accident. Even young children can be taught how to use a telephone. Getting help by using the telephone has been made easier in recent years as more towns and cities set up 911 lines for emergencies.

It's simple. If you need help, dial 911. An operator will answer and you can then describe the emergency, who you are, and where you live. If the system is functioning properly, help should arrive quickly.

If there is no 911 system where you live, then it is important to have police, fire department, and ambulance numbers taped by each phone in the house. If you have a younger brother or sister, make sure they are able to dial or punch in those numbers. And perhaps speak to your parents, guardians, or a teacher at school about starting a 911 service in your community.

Remember, if you are ever in a situation where someone is hurt and there are no adults around, be safe. Make the call for help, even if you aren't absolutely sure it's necessary. Don't take chances when someone's health or life is at stake. It's better to be safe than sorry.

are out playing on a bitterly cold day or get caught in a driving ice storm and can't get to shelter, you might begin to experience hypothermia.

The first symptom of hypothermia is shivering. All of us have shivered from the cold at one time. When that happens, we usually get to a warm place and the shivering stops. But if you can't get to a warm place and your body continues to be chilled, your body begins to give in to the cold.

That means it begins to lower its own temperature. Pretty soon the pulse rate slows and the victim becomes apathetic or indifferent. Then the muscles begin turning rigid and the victim loses consciousness. Hypothermia can happen over a period of several hours or overnight. Or, if someone falls into icy water, hypothermia can occur within minutes.

If someone you know has fallen victim to hypothermia, take the following steps:

1. If the victim is unconscious, call for help. Get an ambulance or someone to take the victim to the hospital immediately.
2. If the victim is conscious, get him to a warmer place as quickly as you can.
3. Wrap the victim with blankets or coats.
4. Give him warm liquids, but never alcohol. Alcohol will give an artificial feeling of being warm, but it won't do the job.
5. Even if he hasn't lost consciousness, suggest that the victim be checked by a doctor.

Hypothermia is not something you need to worry about if you are simply playing football, sleigh riding, ice-skating, or just hanging around during cold weather. If you dress properly, wearing several layers of clothing and a hat, you should be protected. The hat is essential because the largest percentage of body heat is lost from an uncovered head. And once you finish outside, you can usually get to a warm place quickly.

But if you become lost while hiking, fall into icy water, or get soaked by chilling rain and wind, hypothermia becomes a possibility.

FROSTBITE

Frostbite is another by-product of staying out in the cold too long. It happens when a part of the body—usually a hand or

Low temperatures needn't keep you from having fun.
Just dress for the weather and you'll be fine.

foot—has been exposed to very cold air. Frostbite occurs when the cold freezes the tissues of a body part and impairs blood circulation to that part.

Some forms of frostbite can occur very quickly, when you are just shoveling snow or having a snowball fight on a frigid day. Depending on how bad the frostbite is, you may feel stiffness, numbness, and possibly a stinging sensation. The affected skin will look discolored (white, yellow, blue, or flushed).

Mild frostbite, called frostnip, is the least serious type of frostbite, but it does require treatment. Severe frostbite may cause gangrene, an infection that results in the death of tissue because of lack of oxygen. If gangrene does set in, it is sometimes necessary to amputate the affected body part.

If you think you might be getting close to frostbite on your hands or feet, there are a few things you can do. If you can't get inside, you can warm your fingers and hands by placing them under your armpits. That might seem strange, but it's effective because the armpits are always as warm as your body temperature. Or you can roll yourself into a ball. This makes your whole body more heat- and energy-efficient.

Don't rub an area you suspect is frostbitten with snow. Getting it wet will cause you to lose even more heat from the affected area. Heat loss is accelerated by any contact with cold water. If you're with a friend or friends, look at each other's faces. Watch the ears, nose, and cheeks for any noticeable change in color.

Aside from staying indoors, dressing right is the best way to beat the cold. Mittens hold in heat better than gloves. A stocking cap will protect your ears as well as your head. Two pairs of socks and insulated boots will keep your feet warm.

If, despite your precautions, you or a friend should start to show symptoms of frostbite, here's what you should do:

1. Severe frostbite requires immediate medical attention because tissue is dying. While waiting for professional help, you should try to

thaw the affected area as fast as is safely possible. This can be painful. The best way to thaw frostbitten areas is to use warm water in the 100° to 105°F range.

2. Never allow a frostbitten part to refreeze. This will cause even more tissue damage.

3. Even with milder cases, do not rub or put pressure on the frostbitten area. Also don't expose the area to dry heat, such as a stove or fire. Frostbitten areas can be easily burned.

4. Thawing often produces a burning pain. Do not be alarmed by that. Peeling and blistering are also possible with both frostnip and more severe frostbite. Don't break any blisters that may be present.

FIRST-AID MEASURES
YOU SHOULD KNOW

We have talked about having fun while avoiding accidents and injuries. But from time to time, accidents will happen.

If you or a friend suffers an injury, you should be able to recognize the seriousness of that injury and treat it until help arrives. You don't have to be a doctor to do this. You only have to know a few things to look for and then a few basic things to do in response.

LEARN CPR

It's a good idea for everyone to learn CPR. CPR is used to revive someone whose heart has stopped. If CPR is started quickly enough, someone who has been struck by lightning or has had a heart attack or has nearly drowned may be revived.

CPR must be done in two phases. The first is mouth-to-mouth resuscitation, or rescue breathing, which means forcing your breath directly into the victim's mouth and down into the lungs. Phase two is a rhythmic compression of the chest above the heart.

For those who don't feel comfortable giving direct mouth-to-mouth resuscitation, there are two devices available that create a barrier between the rescuer and victim. They are a pocket mask and a rescue key. Both are made of plastic and cover the victim's mouth and nose. The rescuer can then give life-saving breaths without making direct contact with the victim's mouth.

The chest compressions are done between rescue breaths.

This technique must be learned from a trained teacher. Doing it incorrectly, especially with a very young victim, could result in additional injury to the victim. You should also be taught the right way to do mouth-to-mouth. These techniques are not to be taken lightly. They have to be done to a specific rhythm and in conjunction with each other.

Most towns and cities have courses in CPR given by organizations such as the American Red Cross or American Heart Association. Qualified emergency medical technicians may also teach CPR at a local firehouse, first-aid squad, or hospital. Kids as young as ten have learned to perform this lifesaving technique. It's certainly something for you to think about.

HEAD INJURIES

Any head injury should be taken seriously. Signs of a mild concussion include temporary loss of consciousness, emotional instability, and memory loss. Sometimes the victim can't remember how the injury occurred. A more severe concussion can be characterized by the same symptoms, but with a longer period of unconsciousness, plus dilated pupils, a change in breathing, seizures, blurred vision, nausea, bruises around the eyes and ears, and disturbed equilibrium or dizziness.

If someone hits her head in a fall and has any of these symptoms, insist that she remain quiet and get her to a hospital or doctor.

Other possible head injuries include skull fractures, bruising of the brain, and brain hemorrhaging—heavy bleeding within the brain. All these injuries are very serious and should be treated by a professional. Keep the victim quiet, minimize head and spine movement, and maintain an open airway.

NECK INJURY

Unless you are sure that a neck injury is just a sprain, immediate medical attention is required.

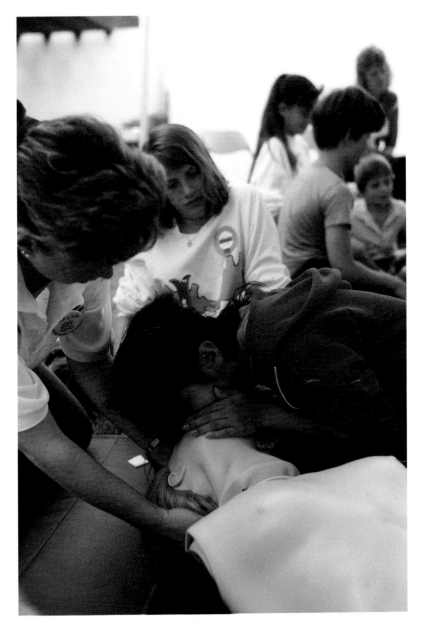

No one knows when they might be called upon to help in an emergency. Learning CPR now is a good way to be prepared for the future.

Don't move someone with a neck injury unless it's to protect them from further danger—moving an injured swimmer out of pounding surf, for instance. This must be done as gently as possible while keeping the victim's neck and spine straight and stable. Never intentionally turn or move the head or neck. Don't bend the person's body. If the injured person is wearing a helmet or other kind of headgear *do not* try to remove it. Keep the victim warm with blankets or anything else that is available. This decreases the chance of shock. Call an ambulance. The victim's neck must be stabilized by a professional before she is moved to minimize any further damage to the spinal cord.

ANKLE SPRAINS

A sprained ankle is a rather common injury. There are several degrees of sprain, some worse than others. Ankle sprains usually occur when you land on the side of your foot and it turns under you. You will feel pain immediately, perhaps severe pain. You may even feel a tearing or popping of the outer part of the ankle.

Talk with an adult—your parent, coach, or guardian. If that adult feels the sprain is mild and you needn't see a doctor, you can treat an ankle sprain with ice packs three or four times a day, twenty minutes at a time. You should also stay off the ankle and keep it elevated as much as possible to reduce the swelling a sprain can cause. If your ankle feels better after seventy-two hours, switch to heat therapy. You can use a heating pad, a hot soak, a hot shower, or heat-producing liniments. If the ankle does not feel better, see a doctor.

Walk as little as possible. Some coaches will recommend crutches for a few days. A sprained ankle is ripe for a re-sprain. So resume your activities slowly and gradually, until all the strength and stability has returned to the ankle. Complete healing may take up to six weeks.

For more serious sprains, a doctor's care is recommended. Sometimes a walking cast is used, followed by taping of the

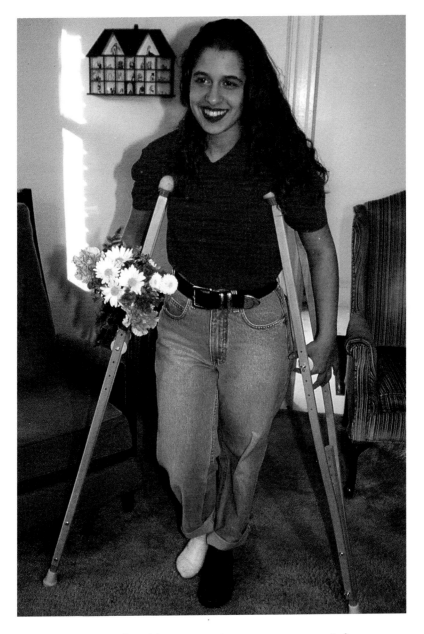

A sprained ankle may put a person on crutches. Recovery time varies from a few days to several months, depending on the severity of the injury.

ankle for support. X rays should always be taken of a serious sprain to check for ligament damage and possible broken bones. A grade 2 sprain may take six to ten weeks to fully heal, while a grade 3 sprain, the most severe, might keep you out of action for twelve to sixteen weeks.

SCRATCHES, CUTS, AND SCRAPES

These are perhaps the most common injuries kids encounter. Many minor scratches, cuts, and scrapes can be ignored until you get home. Some, however, do require immediate attention. And a few even require professional help. Use your head. Always consult an adult if your injury is more than a minor one.

Minor scrapes and scratches should be washed with soap and water once you get home. An antibiotic ointment will prevent any infection from developing.

More serious scrapes rub the outer layer of skin off and can be extensive. Large scrapes must be cleaned thoroughly. If there is dirt or other foreign matter lodged in the injured area, soak it in warm water. This will loosen the dirt so it can be gently rubbed away. Most times, these scrapes do not have to be covered and will heal slowly on their own.

Small, minor cuts do not usually require medical attention. A small cut and the surrounding area should be washed with a mild soap and rinsed thoroughly. After patting it dry, protect the cut with an adhesive-strip bandage. You may also use an antibiotic cream or liquid for added protection and to make the cut heal faster.

Large cuts are another story. The first thing to do is to stop the bleeding. This can usually be accomplished by applying pressure to the wound and elevating the wound above the heart, if possible. Use a handkerchief or other clean cloth. Once the bleeding slows considerably or stops, consult an adult and decide if medical help is needed.

A word of caution about helping someone who is bleeding.

There are a number of dangers in exposing yourself to someone else's blood. Diseases such as AIDS and hepatitis, as well as a number of others, can be transmitted by tainted blood. In addition, germs on your hand can infect the person who is bleeding.

For these reasons, the American Red Cross recommends that people keep a barrier between blood and the hand. If you must put pressure on a bleeding wound and don't have any safety gloves, you can use a plastic bag to cover your hand. You can even use tinfoil, anything that's available that the blood will not penetrate.

If there is nothing available in an extreme emergency and your hand does get in contact with someone's blood, wash it well in soap and water as quickly as possible. And tell a doctor or hospital official just what you did.

If the bleeding will not stop, get help. Have the injured person lie down and try to elevate the wound. This should help to slow the bleeding. If the blood soaks through the first cloth, get another and try again. Do not remove the original cloth. Add the new cloth right on top of the first one.

Some large cuts stop bleeding but must be stitched. Consult an adult to see if stitches are necessary, then get to a doctor or hospital as quickly as possible to have this done. If there is a chance of foreign matter such as glass or metal in the cut, seek medical help. The same advice goes for a cut made with anything rusty or dirty. You may need a tetanus shot under these circumstances.

PULLED MUSCLES

A muscle pull or strain is another common injury that can occur anywhere in the body. You will probably feel a sudden pain in the muscle that will then continue when you try to stretch that muscle or use it again. You may also feel the muscle twitch and you may have some swelling.

Talk to your coach, parent, or guardian. If they agree that

you have a pulled muscle, the muscle should be iced for fifteen minutes three times the first day. The next day begin applying heat. Avoid using the muscle and stay away from the activity that caused the muscle pull. Rest will usually cure the problem. For a mild pull you should heal in two to ten days. A moderate strain will take ten days to six weeks to heal, and a severe strain may need six to ten weeks to heal.

As with sprains, a big problem with a muscle pull is that you will try to do too much too soon. You can then reinjure the muscle and healing will take longer. Stretching before and after exercising is a good way to prevent pulled muscles and to keep muscles loose after they have healed.

All of the recreational activities discussed in this book are fun and enjoyable. The fact that these activities can sometimes lead to accident and injury shouldn't keep anyone from pursuing them.

The trick is to focus on safety. Prepare yourself. Have your body and the equipment you need in tip-top shape. Follow the rules of safety for each activity and don't take foolish chances. A challenge is one thing; a risk is another. Don't let anyone push you into taking a risk. And remember—many accidents can be prevented. By being safety-conscious, you can lower the odds that you, a member of your family, or a friend will ever become an accident statistic.

FURTHER READING

American Red Cross. *Standard First Aid.* St. Louis, Mo.: Mosby, 1993.

Allen, Bob. *Mountain Biking.* Minneapolis, Minn.: Lerner Publications, 1992.

Carter, Sharon. *Coping With Medical Emergencies.* New York: Rosen, 1988.

Clayton, Lawrence. *Everything You Need to Know About Sports Injuries.* New York: Rosen, 1995.

Coombs, Charles. *All-Terrain Bicycling.* New York: Holt, 1987.

Evans, Jeremy. *Hiking and Climbing.* New York: Crestwood House, 1992.

Gutman, Bill. GO FOR IT! series: *Baseball; Basketball; Football; Soccer; Swimming.* New York: Marshall Cavendish, 1990.

——. *Skateboarding.* New York: Tor, 1995.

McGee, Eddie. *The Emergency Handbook.* New York: Simon and Schuster, 1985.

Nielsen, Nancy J. *Bicycle Racing.* New York: Crestwood House, 1988.

Sandelson, Robert. *Swimming and Diving.* New York: Crestwood House, 1991.

Sullivan, George. *In-Line Skating: A Complete Guide for Beginners.* New York: Dutton, 1993.

ORGANIZATIONS TO CONTACT

American Academy of
Orthopaedic Surgeons
P.O. Box 1998
Des Plaines, IL 60017
1-800-824-BONE (2663)
(The *Play It Safe!* program has
several free brochures available.
Ask for *A Guide to Safety for
Young Athletes.*)

American Hiking Society
P.O. Box 20160
Washington, DC 20041-2160
1-301-565-6704

International In-line Skating
Association
Atlanta, GA
1-800-56-SKATE
(Call for a free *Gear Up! Guide to
In-line Skating*, which includes a
directory of certified in-line in-
structors, listed by region.)

International Mountain
Bicycling Association
P.O. Box 7578
Boulder, CO 80306
1-303-545-9011

National Off-Road Bicycle
Association
NORBA
P.O. Box 5513
Mill Valley, CA 94942

National Safety Council
Customer Service
1121 Spring Lake Drive
Itasca, IL 60143-3201
1-800-621-7619

INDEX

PHOTO CREDITS